But Tonight

For Kate,

Happy birthday!

I look forward to

seeing your book soon!

But Tonight

poems by
CJ Martin

mosaic press

Library and Archives Canada Cataloguing in Publication

Martin, CJ, 1966-
    But Tonight / CJ Martin.

Poems.
ISBN 978-0-88962-879-3

    I. Title.

PS8626.A7695B88 2007   C811'.6   C2007-901369-4

Publishing by Mosaic Press, offices and warehouse at 1252 Speers Rd., units 1 & 2, Oakville, On L6L 5N9, Canada and Mosaic Press, PMB 145, 4500 Witmer Industrial Estates, Niagara Falls, NY, 14305-1386, U.S.A.

info@mosaic-press.com

First Printing, March 2007
Second Printing, November 2007

ISBN: 0-88962-879-3
ISBN: 978-0-88962-879-3

Mosaic Press in Canada:	Mosaic Press in U.S.A.:
1252 Speers Road, Units 1 & 2,	4500 Witmer Industrial Estates
Oakville, Ontario	PMB 145, Niagara Falls, NY
L6L 5N9	14305-1386
Phone/Fax: 905-825-2130	Phone/Fax: 1-800-387-8992
info@mosaic-press.com	info@mosaic-press.com

www.mosaic-press.com

".... that exquisite observing of number and measure in the words, and that high-flying liberty of conceit proper to the poet, did seem to have some divine force in it."

Sir Philip Sidney, *A Defence of Poetry*, 1595

Dedications

This book is dedicated to outstanding teachers everywhere, to let you know that what you do is very long-remembered and becomes part of the fibre of those you have taught.

Specifically, this is dedicated the three best teachers at whose feet I personally have had the joy of learning:

Thomas McLaughlin, English Teacher at White Oaks Secondary School, Oakville, Ontario – You laid the foundations of understanding language and literature, and made it incredibly fun and stimulating to learn. You always encouraged me as a thinker and a writer, giving me great marks for disagreeing with you if I could back up my argument. I always looked forward to your classes – which, given that I was a teenager, is the highest compliment you can get!

Professor Maged el Komos, Professor of Cultural Studies, Trent University, Peterborough, Ontario – Your finely-nuanced thinking and clarity of presenting was breath-taking, and called forth my intellectual best-efforts in response. The thought-shifts that occurred while studying with you in many ways affected the path of the rest of my life.

Professor Ellen Cohen, Professor of Comparative Religions, whom I knew while she was at Wilfrid Laurier University, Barrie, Ontario Campus – Your ability to communicate the most subtle concepts of Asian religions transmitted the epiphanies of many lifetimes into your students' consciousness. Even when I was miserably sick and my car was broken, I caught busses to get to your class, as to miss it would have been too great a loss.

Also a special thank you to **Charlotte McRae Arnett**, who taught me in Grade 4. I think you were the first person to recognize that I was a writer. I remember that, without making a big deal of it, you gave me and only me a book of girls' stories as an end-of-year gift, which triggered the question: why did she give this just to me? I knew you were encouraging me for something you saw in me, and even all these thirty-something years later, I thank you for it.

CJ Martin
Oakville, 2007

Acknowledgements

Most Especial Thanks to:

My mother, Mary Frances Martin (fellow poet and my first editor), for being the first person to see almost all of the poems. Thank you for always giving your thoughtful consideration and honest input, which have been invaluable. You have always encouraged and believed in me, and little by little I have become myself.

Rena Sava and Steve Hudak (both visual artists) and everyone else who first initiated the Visual Word Group of poets and painters, through which I started sharing my poetry 'publicly'.

Lyn Estall (artist), the late Donna Penrice (poet and visual artist), Stella Body (poet), Brenda Boisvert (arts activist), Stephen Marvin (musician and the most poetic novelist I've ever read) for their particularly enthusiastic encouragement.

Sylvia Collins (poet), for being someone with whom I have enjoyed 'workshopping' poems, and whom I always trust to show new material.

Sean Levine (truly the greatest comic genius of our generation), for being an advocate, champion and nurturer of my creative growth and expression.

Catherine Mondragon (film-maker), whose speaking-voice reading my material is more like the voice I hear in my head than my own voice is. At some point we will finish the CD-version of this!

Patrick Woodcock (poet and editor), first, for making me get rid of so much material ("It's a hideous conjoined twin – you gotta cut it off!"), and then for hearing each remaining poem so sensitively. Your intuition on what to improve was always right on.

Emma Bramma Smith (artist), whose artwork, unlike my own visual art, manifests the exact same *spirit* as some of my poems. Your illustrations for *For Kind Melinda's Pains* are perfect, and I can't wait to be able to present our work on that poem together as a fully illustrated manuscript in its own right.

Heather Morgan of Lifespark Photography (www.lifespark. ca), for adding her photographic creativity to this project. You quickly captured many aspects of me, although we have just recently met.

Howard Aster, of Mosaic Press, for his kind help in bringing this work to the world.

And I would be remiss not to thank Tom, Wolf, Kerry and LaLa for your patience when mommy was not petting you – I know it must have seemed inexplicable that I could sometimes find a blank page more interesting that a live cat!

ONE

But Tonight

There will come a time
When the moon will not exist
And the sun will have given up its form
To lose itself in nothingness,
And all that we now dream on
Will have slid to shadow.

But tonight

Moonlight dances
On the fading Autumn leaves
And caresses the smooth skin
Of the responsive lake

And I have you in my arms

And the air is sweet
With the scent of things falling away.

Drowsing

I love this moment
When gravity
Becomes triple-strength
And a cocoon
Knits itself
Around my inertia.

I surrender.

Soon I will dissolve
And become
My own essences
Inside a quiet sack.

I let this heaviness
Take me in,
Where I fall,
Freely,
Away
From myself

Landing
With wings outstretched
On a beautiful bud
Of oblivion.

Triangulating

There's a fire in my soul
That I want the world to see

There's a woman dancing round it
'Neath the stars in naked glee

There's a song triangulating
Twixt the Flame and Flame and Flame

Of a Fire and a Cosmos
And a Woman with a Name.

Church Bells

Church bells in the night
And the light snow falling.

Church bells?
The resonating sound
Catches my breath -
An instant reminder
Of my indivisibility,
My infinite community,
Of history, eternity.

Church bells
Calling all afar:
"I'm here,
Still here."

Church bells
And the soft grey blue
Snow-sky
Wrapping overhead
Like a stroking hand.

Church bells
Ringing across the valleys

So that even a wanderer like me
Can hear the voice of God
Carried over the winter drifts.

Change

We can try to hold on
To previous patterns,
Like a child afraid
Of the irreversibility of turning thirteen.

We can stand with empty hands
That once dripped
With gems and flowers,
Without the currency of the foreign land
Whose shore is fast-approaching.

The ocean beats its pulse-rhythm
Into the resistant rock
Turning it to sand so fine
That the shy sun
Peeping over the water
Cannot recognize the place
Where she had been --

Except in certain colours,
Certain vibrations,
And the melancholy joy
Of molecular structure
That remains unchanged
As its song escapes from a broader surface.

At the atomic level,
Electrons care not
If they are in grain or cliff.

Old Boat

Sea-brine and time
Combine
To crack
Her thin
Polymer skin

Steady-on,
She slides
Her aging beauty
Through the rough tides

Weathered and unashamed
She sails westward

Carrying salt
For luck

Abandoning pride
For joy

The wild-fire sky
Licks her wounds

Soul Looks Up

Soul looks up

undersides of wings
soaring wide-sky'd by

the shadow-space
where impalpable air is cupped
and transformed to climbing, gliding power

Soul look in

and all that
once seemed

empty

now shows
the possibility
of flight

12:01 AM

One minute old is this new day -
So strange it happens in the dark;
Long hours to endure after its start,
Groping feebly on weak young legs,
Hoping to find a crack of dawn
To wedge its infant fingers in
And test its strength.

Born in blindness, how does it know
A sun exists to be wrenched out?

Abandoned

Abandoned
The silent shell
Sinks to the bottom
Of a shallow channel

Its whitish, glimmering concavity
Staring up
Through the shifting water
To the brightness beyond.

Silt and sand
Slowly flow in,
Lining its slopes,
Lingering in the ridge-edges.

Gravity works its seduction.

The grains
Will only leap
And leave
If the right current descends
At the right angle...

But such a current never comes.

The winds move the waterskin
But half-buried below,
The shell lives only the changes
Of light to dark

Feeling the dull caress
Of motion too general to disturb

Until at last it believes
It was meant only to hold sand.

Autumn Leaves

Autumn leaves have blown in
Through my open door.

They strew the floor.

And I find
I do not rush
To find a vacuum;

I do not brush
Them back outside.

Last Will of Spring's great work
Finding rest within my four walls,

I am honoured
The wind chose
To bring you here.

The Electron Chant

Stones and rocks with atoms bright
Microcosmic angel light
Flight in frozen-seeming hills
Deeper freeing might that thrills
Singing, spinning dance of life
Pulsing joy beneath the strife

Stones and rocks with atoms bright
Microcosmic angel light
Flight in frozen-seeming hills
Deeper freeing might that thrills
Singing, spinning dance of life
Pulsing joy beneath the strife

Stones and rocks with atoms bright
Microcosmic angel light
Flight in frozen-seeming hills
Deeper freeing might that thrills
Singing, spinning dance of life
Pulsing joy beneath the strife

Stones and rocks with atoms bright
Microcosmic angel light
Flight in frozen-seeming hills
Deeper freeing might that thrills
Singing, spinning dance of life
Pulsing joy beneath the strife

(Repeat, in simple barefoot circle-dance)

Old Words

There is a life to every word
Now it is spoke -- now it's unheard;
And what becomes of such as these
Who live as echoes in the breeze?

"Honour" must be counted thus:
Its radiant gleam is now but rust;
And "Chastity", whose youth was proud,
Is hardly ever said aloud.

"Sacrifice", a virtue high,
Is suspiciously regarded by
Those who've rightly come to fear
A controlling speaker draweth near.

"Character", a cause to love,
Is very seldom heard above
The cry for what is new and fresh
And current focus on the flesh.

Sweet "Freedom" now is still bespoke,
But, sadly, has become a joke --
As trapped within our latest words
More freeing phrases pass unheard.

The Old Way of Dancing

Weave a magic
Hand to hand
No strangers here
No strangers here

Smiling rhythms, step, step
Balance, swing your neighbour, step
Eyes meet eyes, too long, look away
Meet again, step, smile, step

Weave a magic
Hand to hand
No strangers here
No strangers here

Gents do an alleman
One and a half
Ladies, swaying, watching, step
Ready, join the pattern, step

Weave a magic
Hand to hand
No strangers here
No strangers here

Face your partner
Long-line-step
One dance, one music, step and step
Side by side, one movement, step

Weave a magic
Hand to hand
No strangers here
No strangers here

Haiku #2

Music of the Spheres
Echoing in my garden -
Universe in bloom.

Haiku #8

I am the small shell
In which the ocean echoes
Its cry for the moon.

Haiku # 10

Dust gathers, hides shine -
Luster's lost to lack of time;
Dullness settles in.

Haiku # 12

Silence fills midnight,
A held breath suspends the sky,
Starlight slides through time.

Haiku # 16

Always there is joy:
On days when the sun is hid
Water's life is known.

Haiku # 17

Inner springs are tapped -
Words tumble up like water -
The desert page blooms.

Haiku # 24

Burn, sacred flame, burn --
Turn my blood gift to soul smoke
Soaring back to sky.

Haiku # 28

Mountain steep, clouds low;
We climb blind; creeping; but proud;
Growing. Keeping vows.

Haiku # 34

This old frame watches
Captures time, highlights small change,
Cups seasons gently.

Haiku # 37

Moved from shade to sun
The near-dead tree starts anew,
Rebuilds, unfurls, grows.

Haiku #42

Distant, detail dims,
Essential shapes emerge bare -
Undisguised, pure form.

Haiku # 45

Blood is air and sun -
Oh sacred complexity,
Whose depths are simple.

Haiku # 53

Crawling, tentative,
Crumpled, yet free, in night breeze,
Old news-sheets blow by...

Haiku # 59

All things fade away
Fullness empties; motion stills –
Leaves no trace, just space

Haiku # 60

Walls broken, roof gone
That room where babes were conceived
Now rotting. Winds blow.

Haiku # 62

Three years without rain -
Green flesh like a monument
Holding on to hope

Haiku # 65

Boys gossip past me.
Invisible in plain view;
Middle-aged; "other".

TWO

Current

Water rushes
Cascading with a crash
On rocks so thick
They sit like gods
Laughing in the face
Of the unabating force

While I, fragment, wisp,
Bound in small
By this thin confine of skin
Ache to touch
The life flow
Surging by

Too fragile
To sit in its roar
Or travel its path,
I press my body
Against the cool, damp bank
Trail my fingers
In the charging current
And let the energy
Tear apart
My separateness

Baptizing myself
In its strength
Until I feel my spirit stream

The River Calls

The river calls
Its ancient pathway answers
Echoes ripple down ·
The land's edge
Washing back into the flow
That tore and wore
The rock cleaved through
With its insistence

The earth calls
Its coursing water hearkens
Searching around every bend
Slowly removing all obstacles
Always seeking
Never finding
The place to rest
And listen
To the whisper
Of its name

Spreads Like the Sun

Slow, still, floating
Gliding along the breath of wetland
Where heron wings cup the air
And brush the tips of cattails
And wild marsh flowers

Water suspends itself in a moment of knowing,
Rises, bridges the chasm between earth and sky

Silence flows, rolling gently
With the sun-gloss fluid always there already gone

Trees take their fill of summer
Resting calmly in the fullness of themselves
And in the quietness of the windless air replete

Serene the lives of each shine
'Til glow on glow the radiance dazzles

I spin my kayak
And feel the reeling life looping around me and into me
My breath so calm and my mind so loose
It spreads like the sun and caresses the surfaces
And inner selves of the living landscape

I am a ripple under my paddle
I am a small tough leaf feeding lake-bottom roots
I am the stillness of the cattails, motionless in their multitudes
Stretching skyward in the undulating hush

Sediments

I stand a fleeting instant on a vast outcrop of Time
My transient foot flicks passing rock as up the slope I climb --
Some massive Force heaved heavenward a million years gone by
And settled, torn, serene, a mile closer to the sky.

A thousand years or more have humans come unto this place
To gather food, take shelter, or t'absorb the rugged grace
And few have failed to wonder at the age of this huge range
And seen in rock and avalanche the signs of ancient change.

Oh, how the sight of Time itself, laid bare, for all to see,
Can lift the mind beyond a sense of its own history
To dwell if for a moment with the Powers that had seethed
And crushed a continent before these mighty mountains breathed.

And then we're shaken by the thought of Powers gone before
That layered grain on grain along more ancient ocean's floor
Some silent, patient Force of Will a *b*illion years gone by
That slowly built Itself a mile closer to the sky.

Muskoka Pine

Gnarled roots splaying
Along the rough granite
Anchoring into any crack
Where soil can settle,
Stretching its search
Over a wide, snaking circumference,
Seeking the rains,
Running all across
A hard, bare land
Where only the determined survive

For A Setting Moon

A hint of orange upon the pond
Is all that tells of your fair night --
And now that you have all but gone
None could tell you'd been so bright.

I've watched you since you first did rise,
So full and perfect in your strength --
Your radiant beams lit up the skies
And stretched out to their fullest length.

Then drew you close to kiss the pond,
More intimate in your descent,
Lingered low, but not for long,
Bade farewell and softly went.

And who will know, with the dawn
Arising from their dreaming sleep,
That all night long your brilliance shone
And penetrated darkness deep?

Still, tomorrow night you'll come
To trace anew your path of light,
Until again you do become
A hint of orange at end of night.

Rainkist

Soft does drizzle down dark night slide
It kisses at the grasses
And the ducks become its bride
It caresses all the faces
In the patient dim hillside
And the warmth of it surpasses
All the sun has ever tried.

Immanence

Many times the moon has traced
Her path across the sky
As with the distant stars she raced
Grew full, grew wane and died.

The falling dance of ancient lights
From galaxies unknown
Have always told of cosmic might --
But I was as a stone.

But now, to sleep under the stars
And gaze unto the heaven
Is to feel the closeness of the far
And with all to be brethren.

Do Not Into Houses Go

When the sun has sunken low
Do not into houses go --
Stay amid the roots of trees
And taste the many-scented breeze.

When the moon begins to rise
Let no roof block out the skies --
Listen for the lunar sighs
And let nothing that sound disguise.

When the stars above take wing,
Ritually circling --
Be still! Perceive the night's rich lore!
Do not put thyself indoors.

When distance stands dark silhouette
Do not into parlours get --
Let eyes and feet and soul go free
Partaking in the majesty.

Lessons from the Annelids

In darkened world beneath the sod
A rich life live the lowly worms
I doubt they have a sense of God
But happily live on their own terms.

A tail have they to move them on,
And sensitive skin to draw upon
To tell them all they need to know--
And having this they live and grow.

And if by chance they cast a thought
On what they have and they have not
In the world which is their home
They'd fancy they are paragon.

No eyes have they to see me stand
With my garden spade in hand;
No ears to hear my master plan
For this grassy piece of land.

Their confident blindness makes me ponder
And of ourselves I'm forced to wonder
Is it but human arrogances
To claim a world with just five senses?

The Green Word

The green word is uttered
Unfurling itself ceaselessly
Water, air, transitory forms and beings
Sliding endlessly through each other
Within our parental sun's embrace

The green word is uttered -
Can you hear it?

Go deep into the forest
Find a place where the grass
Is soft under your fingertips
Place your back against the oldest tree
Close your eyes
Calm your mind
And listen
For the sound
Of your own
Breath.

Haiku #3

Cool, sweet, fertile air
Breathes newborn flower-secrets
Into yearning blood.

Haiku #5

A-light from within,
The impassioned, red-hot tree
Brands the air with joy.

Haiku #6

Soft green, now; calmer;
Spring's bright blaze full-spent, content,
This year's grasses fade.

Haiku #7

Pleasure? Surprising:
A crisp orange day still pleases,
After all these years.

Haiku # 9

Smooth slip of blue silk
Wrapping beauty in soft shades --
Loose-draped morning sky.

Haiku # 11

Elegant white sleeves
Grace the limbs of bowing trees --
Night-woods now formal.

Haiku # 13

More precious than gems,
Magic water-beads adorn,
Then become, young leaves.

Haiku # 18

Two birds balancing,
Swaying so symmetrically
On thin, twin twigs: sing!

Haiku # 20

Leaves grow, fade, fall, bud -
The real tree lies underground,
Endures; strong, hidden.

Haiku # 22

Vast sapphire aglow --
Earth's blue blood, alive. Endless
Tide of majesty.

Haiku # 23

Blaze of living song --
Splays of palm fronds five feet long --
Calm days traced, heat-graced.

Haiku # 25

Wood's mournful voice creaks,
Calls out from cell memories
To those still living.

Haiku # 26

Sunflower children
Forfeit their futures for his,
Become this bird's song.

Haiku # 29

Frost's capricious play
Reveals water's artful wit,
Delights, then melts 'way.

Haiku # 31

Blue tints and shadows,
Snow stretches, dozes, wrapped in
Sunless morning sky.

Haiku # 32

Fighting through black night
Thousands, millions, countless, white
Snow conquers, brings light.

Haiku # 39

Floating ribbon path
Purposed curiosity
The bee stops, tastes, darts.

Haiku #43

Dull bones break their doze
Marrow flows like memory -
Spring calls all that lives

Haiku #47

Night splits, forced open -
Brief glimpses of life's light guide
Through these short, cold days.

Haiku # 49

Deep black sky transforms -
Planetary spin's revealed
In pale-shifting shades.

Haiku # 52

Lean wolf, pale-breathed, cold,
Scans the dawn stillness for life
Which will become his

Haiku # 54

Magnetism plays,
Drawing migrational maps
High above the land.

Haiku # 56

Blow wind – bounce branches
Bursting with abundant life
Fling buds ope' – spread Spring!

Haiku # 57

Night falls, voices call
From hidden places. This life –
Needs not sun but moon.

Haiku # 58

Still water reflects
Sky, leaves, world outside, above...
Deeper, creatures stroll.

THREE

Oh, Who Can Paint

Oh, who can paint the colours of true love?
What tint can capture light that radiates
Pure joy? What final form uncomplicates,
Unfolds, undoes the mysteries whereof
Two souls unite as if some force above
Had made each to fulfill the other's fates?
And how can texture tell the hidden traits
Of fullness feeling found when hand meets glove?

'Tis quite beyond the reach of mortal man
To tell another soul what love reveals;
Yet strive we on with high ambitious plan
To be the brave Prometheus who steals
From Heaven's realm that gift of holy flame
By which to show the meaning of Love's name.

While Passion Bids

My lover's eyes are not divine; his gaze
Does not within me stir the primal fire;
Nor does his visage pondered bring desire
So savage-sweet I burn with holy craze.

Oh! Keenly do the feelings of malaise
Come, craving bliss that dwells in heavens higher,
Above the earthly soot and daily mire
Where Being sings to Love eternal praise.

And while I sit surrendered to alarm
With all my inner world in disarray,
He comes to me and wraps me in his arms
So soft in strength   I marvel at his way
Of taking me to places safe and warm
While Passion bids me leave without delay.

Life Partnering

I would not have thee be my King
For Queen is subject under him
And power is an ugly thing
That makes Love's lustre grow too dim.

I would not have thee be my god,
The essence of my very being --
My soul would recognize the fraud
And from false capture soon go fleeing.

I would not have thee be my sun,
The source and font of all of life --
For where the wild deer do run
'Tis nature plays both drum and fife.

But I would take thee by the hand
In knowledge and in innocence
And crown thee with a golden band
And have thee as my only Prince.

Unsaid

Flowing unsaid
Over the words
And under the tone

(it reaches me)

Hovering in the thick air
Through this oversized room

(it pulls me)

Balancing delicately
On roles and rules

(it shakes me)

Feeling its way towards
Revelation or extinction

(it caresses me)

Watchful, cautious,
Ready to retreat

(it captures me)

Measures exposure
Makes its escape

Single Girl's Song

Here I am, Here I am, Here I am, Where *Are* You?

This is where I live now. This is where I eat my meals. This is where I slide my socks along the hardwood floor and dream of the ballrooms of old Quebec...

I have done it up quite well, they say. The rose and cream create a relaxing ambience and the couch is very sinksome.

I have made a chandelier out of an old fixture. I have put many hours into making the yard bear fruit.

I have an ever growing library, and a tub deep enough to wrap me entirely like a warm blanket. On the ceiling above it I have painted a Celtic mandella.

I go to the gym twice a week and am no longer ashamed of my thighs. I play volleyball, and have people to drink beer with after the game.

I have a special room for writing and painting and drinking wine at 3:00 am on a work night.

I am the girl in the woman's body, the girl in the woman's heart, the youthful hope that dares to creep about the dim heaviness of experience saying Here I am, Here I am, Here I am, Where *Are* You?

I make car payments and have health insurance. I made my first **RRSP** deposit at age 31. I am paying down my debts and wavering between a trip abroad and a house deposit.

I am collecting the hair that I comb from my cat, to make a blanket. I don't want to own a dog right now. I feel safe enough in this neighbourhood.

I am making it, making my way, making due, making ends meet, making it up as I go along, making a home for myself, but

In the silence that sounds between the footfalls and in the silhouettes that play against the dinner party walls, I see and hear the whispered thought

Here I am, Here I am, Here I am, Where *Are* You?

Climax

C-l - -!
The explosive beginning
A sudden break of breath long held
Expelled
In a crashing rush
That leads to a cry
I-I-I
Sharp and high as a fever
On a blistering night
Shrill as a wild song
Piercing darkness
Calling, responding
I, I
Am
I am, I ammmmm
mmm-m
The delicious
Knowledge of self
Fully alive
Settling into the velvet depths
Tasting through the skin
m-mm-m....
then a-a-ah
the long moan
that mourns
that knows this is already passing
utters itself gutterally
sweetly savouring the sweat
that soaks it
as the moment
drains away
slowly
in a final, frictionless Xssss

Firemoth

Would that I could meld with you, flame alight -
My wings burn bright
And casting sparks
Draw poor other moths, like me

Feeling their palpitations
Dying vainly at my side
I am the bride of all their sorrows
I wed their pain to my tomorrows

Firemoth that I am,
Too burnsome to them
And blinded by you

The Stain of This

This moment gapes
Like a fresh, raw wound,
Its blood surging and seeping

I long to escape
From the pitiful sound
Of my own weeping

Darkness comes; it drapes
Me in blue-blacks profound;
And this wake I am keeping

Mauls the breath
From all I know
Nothing can grow
In the stain of this death

What Isn't

Bodies press together

After the salt-sweet grip
Even during

Eyes look, but don't meet

Close, cannot forget

Glimpses of what isn't

The Closet of Childless Mothers

In the closet of childless mothers
Sympathy stands on its head --
And the sighs and the tears
It will shed through the years
Are reserved for the moms of the dead.

In the closet of childless mothers
Another crowd keeps out of view:
They're ashamed of their grief
As it meets unbelief
Though their mourning is equally true.

In the closet of childless mothers
Portions of many of us dwell;
And though we do fine,
Make careers, wine and dine,
Deep parts of us still go through hell.

Oh the closet of childless mothers
Is filled with the rubber and Pill
That made us feel free
But changed destiny
And whose "safety" now fails to fulfill.

In the closet of childless mothers
We women of freedom abound.
And we watch, mouths agape
As the thing we escaped
Proves the thing that we most wanted found.

There's a closet of childless mothers,
It's packed full of pain that's ignored;
And each babe that goes by
Tells that part of us died --
Keep that death in the closet, close-doored.

He Gardens Me

My lover's eyes reveal his caring soul,
So fully does he drop pretense and guile.
Unselfishly he gives his open smile
And holds me close, and has no other goal.

When morning calls us each to play our role
He bids it wait for just a little while
To kiss my face and hair and lips so I'll
Not go to face my dragons less than whole.

What strength he gives with gestures small but kind
That tell and show me what love means to him
And let me see the corners of his mind
Where doting thoughts do overflow the brim!
What flower wouldn't thrive under such care?
He gardens me. I think God answers prayer.

FOUR

Not Enough Nelly

Not-Enough-Nelly has a large, empty belly
She thinks it'd be swell if you'd feed her all day
You can feed her your income, your passions, fair dinkum!*
You can feed her all the things that you do and you say -
You can give her your home, your vacation, your nation
She'll take it impatiently, all your best stuff;
She'll look at you blankly and tell you "Quite frankly,
I've had better elsewhere; well it's just not enough."

You can buy bigger houses and catch younger spouses
Or spouses who are thinner, or smarter or rich
You can dress with more power and work out by the hour
And do all that you need to be top of your niche -
You can get great big raises and garner high praises
But all of their words will soon wash down the drain
Cuz Nelly is louder and she's not any prouder
And you'd see she was starving "if you had half a brain."

You've made strides in great causes? But the applause
Isn't heard over top of old Nelly's demands;
You're awarded top prizes, but the surprise is
That none of it sticks, it slides straight through your hands
And into the maw of this Not-Enough monster
Whose voice only taunts you and then commands "More!"
You can give her your Oscar, your Nobel, your Juno
She'll look through you, you know, and say "You're a bore."

Not-Enough-Nelly has a terrible belly
It doesn't have anything there that digests!
Things pass right through her then she needs something newer
And she'll eat you yourself if you take any rests!
Or will she? Well, can she? She's only a figment
That lives in your head that you've nurtured and fed
And helped to grow stronger - well, not any longer!
I tell you it's time that old Nelly was dead!

For she's got you careening for lack of all meaning
She's eaten your life, and your hope and your peace -
There can be no fulfillment when all of your will's bent
On heeding and feeding a bottomless beast.

No! Old Nelly is hollow, so don't let her swallow
The big dreams and small things that make up your year...
Just find your own center, and so, circumvent her -
You'll smile at the fullness you see in the mirror.

*Note for non-antipodeans: Fair dinkum is Aussie slang for "genuine", "really",
"truly" or "for real".

Old-Fashioned Recipe For The Un-Created Self

First, take one fresh-squeezed soul;
Cover in ashes and coffee grounds;
Bury deep within a mound of chores;
Let ferment;
Check on it every year or two.

Warning: Foulness may emanate.

Calls the Nightbird

Calls the nightbird sweetly
From a branch I cannot see,
In a voice so soft and lowly,
"Take one step and follow me."

Drops the cliff edge steeply
Plunging down into the sea,
Where the water's hurly-burly
And no human-kind can be.

Calls the nightbird plainly
And I know it's calling me,
In this place so shadowed darkly:
"Take one step and follow me."

Falls the dark so thickly
Hiding well that horrid tree,
Where the nightbird waits serenely
For my choice which must be free.

Calls the nightbird keenly,
In a voice that's edged with glee,
Gloating o'er it's bone collection,
"Take one step and follow me."

Who Can Stand?

Blood and dust
Mingle murkily
Running down
To hide their shame,
Trailing through
The once-calm-clarity

Stormclouds take up arms
And overthrow
The weakening sun
Roaring their victory
To the darkened, deafened earth

All that they have won
Begins to pale
Growth becomes decay
Paradise weeps
To watch itself sicken
For who can bide
The dirges
Blowing in the rank wind?

Cancer covers all
Roses shyly hide
Their grotesque forms
Creatures starve themselves
To cease their witness
For none can bear
The painful memory of hope

"When Sin claps his broad wings
Over the battle
And sails rejoicing
In the flood of Death,
O who can stand?"·
Silence answers
In the pitiful spaces
Between the thunder's booms

* After William Blake's "Lullaby"

By An English Grave

In twilight mists of times long past
There lived an English country lass.
I know but this about her life:
Some torment deep was in her rife.

When she was in her sixteenth year,
Some grief unquenchable by tear,
Some overwhelming sense of fear,
Brought sharpened knife through bosom clear.

Because the hand had been her own
In death no mercy was she shown:
Not welcome she within the gates
With those who met less woeful fates.

Sickness, murder, accident, age,
None of these do so enrage,
But one whose solitary crime
Was to stop the hands of time
When in a state of disaffection
Is branded e'er with God's rejection.

Surely now she's all but gone,
Save for hair, and save for bone,
And save a fading, weathered stone
Left on a grave that's all alone.

Now there is a road well-trod
That parts her separated clod
Farther from the reach of kin
Like further penance for her sin.

'Tis fairly overgrown with grass --
No care for her unto the last,
Who lived in twilight times long past,
A saddened, maddened country lass.

FIVE

Goldfish

I had Goldfish for breakfast
And a cup of instant brew;
I haven't shopped for weeks now -
Surprising? Well, it's true.
My cupboard's bare as lizard bones
In arid desert heat;
My carpet's grown an extra coat
And it's hard to find a seat
That isn't stacked with something
Like books, or socks or junk...
A shrink would diagnose me
As being in a funk
But the blues are not the culprit
In this chaos and neglect:
A fit of writing's got me
And I really don't object
To popcorn as a main course,
And as long as I have tea
The daily chores can wait a month -
I'm tending the real me.

I Thought I Saw An Ibis

I thought I saw an ibis
As I drove along the road
It was standing on the corner
It was stretching as it strode

And I looked at it in wonder
And I looked with sudden thrill
For not often does a driver
See an ibis in Oakville

And as I glimpsed its graceful neck
I transported to the Nile
Where its kindred preened in clusters
Silhouetted 'gainst the dial

Which shone in tropic brilliance
As it slid into the mud
Where the greenest slips were sprouting
Newly wakened by the flood

And a sense of awe infused me
As I lost my sense of time
For the ibis is eternal
And its nature is sublime

It had flown before the Pharaohs
Ever gained the thought of power
It had lived in simple magic
Never thinking of its hours

All this in just a second
Then my focus got more fine
And I saw my enchanting ibis
Was in fact a tattered sign

But Tonight - CJ Martin

But was I disappointed
At the stick and sagging scrap
Whose motion in the morning breeze
Had blown me across the map?

Oh no indeed - it thrilled me more
To know a ragged sign
Was enough to spawn a pondering calm
And animate my mind.

The Reservation

"Trays noch-es" I said slowly,
"Merta... Junio...Bientay Nuay-ba"
Three nights, Tuesday June 29 -
OK
There, I'd said it
All my Spanish,
All at once.

Her response:
"Mrava ahutio whammo flava flora fauna?
Mrava, si? Quebilliato con something or other...

Oh God Oh God Oh God Oh God
My phrasebook laying limp in my hand
As helpful as a dead parrot.

"Merta... Junio...Bientay Nuay-ba"
I try again, clearer, slower

She slows, tries to give me options
"Macremondo bogania quesa possa, si?
Solo grecko gecko flamingo..."

Squeaking, I assert again
"Merta... Junio...Bientay Nuay-ba?"
Tuesday June 29.

She pauses. She repeats
"Bientay Nuay-ba."

"Si!" I exclaim. "Si! Gracias!"

"Gracias," she says

I hang up,
Triumphant!

Then realize
I've booked the wrong day.

Oh'd to the Pain that Lives in My Back

When summer dawn twinkles
And sparkles with dew
I lie without moving
Lest I should wake you.

Oh sleep, tireless worker,
Take rest, be at ease;
Forget me for two
Minutes more, if you please.

I won't be offended,
No, no, that's just fine!
I'll lie here and guard it,
Your object, my spine.

You lie there, I promise
I won't go away
(Even as I say this
My legs start to stray...

Just a few more maneuvers
And I'll be out of bed...)
But oh! Now you've got me!
From my knees to my head.

How quickly you waken!
Good morning, back pain.
No need for such hurry -
There's nothing to gain

Come faster or slower
You always achieve
Your ends even better
Than Fagan can thieve.

———————— But Tonight - CJ Martin ————————
73

No small praise! You're a pro!
I salute you! I do!
For sheer dedication
There's no one like you.

So! Where will we start
In our next daily rounds
Of battling it out
O'er my body, this ground.

I'll start with the stretches,
You throw in your best
Shots of spasms and stabbings
And then we'll both rest.

We'll take tea on the porch
While you work up your strength
And when we get up
You'll stretch out to full length.

Oh I know you, you codger,
Same old you and me -
Companions, opponents
Experienced are we!

A Toast

The daughters of the grapeseed in their green glass dresses stand
As the sons of father Hopfield to Sir Barley lend a hand;
They go frequently to parties and the times they make are grand,
And all is as it should be in our happy-throated land!
So come ye merry revelers and harken this command:
To and with these lads and lasses with your glasses raise your hand!

SIX

Illustration by Emma Bramma Smith

For Kind Melinda's Pains – A Romance for Young Readers

Prefatory imaginings:
First, a storm-tossed ocean; several tall ships are being hurled into the foreground; one ship, in the distance, is going down.

Second, a wharf, with several beleaguered ships, and one vacant slip; the shivering people on the docks hear the news of the loss of one of the fleet. Melinda is on the dock among them. (Turn the page....)

The names of all the souls aboard
Reach pale Melinda's ears
Like sounds unrecognized; unmoored,
One name alone she hears.

Towards her home she rushes, lo!
See how she struggles on
As fierce November winds do blow
Her tears into the storm.

Her head, so lovely, arches back
In anguish under heaven;
Her arms, like children's, seem to lack
The strength that they were given;

Her heart is broke, her soul in pain
"Why Willie, Lord," she cries –
She cries the same, again, in vain
"Why Willie, Lord, not I?"

The loss of love is hard to bear
When love is all your life;
And fair Melinda only cared
To be young Willie's wife.

———— But Tonight - CJ Martin ————

See others in the streets – look there!
The running, soakéd shapes
That leap o'er puddles, pulling close
The collars of their capes.

See how they pull their focused gaze
To just beyond their feet
And fail to see those in a daze
Of pain on their same street.

No gentle hand extends to her
No arm will guide her safe:
She is alone now in the world
Instead of wife, a waif.

See how the blur of boots whiz past
Another hapless soul,
Who huddles down for shelter poor
Within a muddy hole.

No cape nor coat protects this lad
His shirt drips wet and cold
He wonders if he'll even live
To see sixteen years old.

His breath comes sharp; his body shakes;
He's numb in hands and feet;
His legs are thin as marker stakes;
He has nothing to eat.

"Kind sir!" he gasps as feet go by,
"Excuse me, sir, I'm cold!"
But no one seems to hear his cries;
No mercy sweet is doled.

"Excuse me, miss!" he tries again:
Feet stop, a face looks down;
He sees a girl with tear-stained cheeks,
She kneels upon the ground.

"Please miss," he says, his voice now pleads,
"I have no place to go."
His eyes avert, ashamed to be
Seen sunken down so low.

"Then come and stay with me," she says
"Then come and stay with me;
For I am now a widow made,
My love is with the sea."

Then reached she down and pulled him up
And on him threw her shawl;
She led the lad through winds a-foul
Into her own front hall.

Look there, beyond the row of pegs
Where Willie's coat is not:
The lonely room weeps emptily
Around their double cot.

See how Melinda's shoulders bear
The weight of the strange lad;
Her steps advance them both for he
Has lost what strength he had.

His eyelids flicker closed and ope',
And closed again, but try
To hold onto his consciousness
Against his fever high.

What spectacle beneath the moon
Could more have stirred the heart
Than one soul's pain held in restraint
When called to play her part.

See how she puts the unknown lad
Upon the empty bed
Then lights a fire and goes to find
Her towel for his head.

And in an hour's time the lad
Is dry, the room is warm.
Melinda sits alone – he sleeps—
She stares into the storm.

Oh Heaven sweet, be kind to those
Whom Love has called her own;
A fragile thing becomes the heart
When hope has fully flown.

Melinda's mouth repeats the word
Her mind can barely own -
How can a mind know true the weight
Of little words like 'gone'.

She twists her auburn tresses round
And round about her hand;
With all that's left inside of her
She tries to understand;

For not quite three full times the moon
Has waxed and waned and died
Since she at Larkspur altar had
Become dear Willie's bride.

And now! See how the moon's lost too
No light Melinda sees;
All flooding, blurring, pounding does
November bring its freeze;

All chilling, numbing, fading creeps
A winter bleak and long;
"No end, no end to winter's deep;
Nowhere will I belong."

See how the lad upon the bed
Turns left his head, then right;
And look upon his furrowed brow,
All troubled in the night;

His breath comes sharp and fast, his eyes
Close tight against the pain;
His body young has come unstrung,
His strength now fully drained.

Melinda hears his low-breathed moan --
What pain to her it gives!
My Willie's gone, she says, but oh!
By God, I'll see he lives!

A tiny spark of light she bears
Beside his fitful bed;
A pale and teared Melinda vows
The lad won't join the dead.

She practices the ancient arts
Both subtle and obscure,
With herbs and heats and bandagings
And potions that will cure.

And as she tends, Melinda sees
Within the lad's young face
The feelings that she knew so well
Are now his saving grace.

For in his eye a look of love
For someone far away
Do seem to make him struggle on
To see another day.

Melinda nods her head, and sings
In low and soothing tones
The tunes of love the young lad needs
To soothe his spirit's moans.

Hark - calmer, softer, comes his breath;
His brow has hopeful lines;
Melinda's soul is in each note
As heart within her pines.

"Oh, Willie," says she, silently,
"Shall never more I sing
My songs of love to make the moon
The gift to you I bring?"

And when her voice within her fails
She hums, if weakly, on,
To carry on her melodies
His soul into the dawn.

All through the night the fire's lights
Watch, witnessing the wonder
Of healing flowing from a heart
So fully torn asunder.

Behold – how quiet seems the lad,
More restful now he lays;
His fever broke, his body still,
His voice he tries to raise:

"My Anne," the young lad breathes the name
His being needs the most;
"She waits for you," Melinda chants,
As if to Willie's ghost.

Full gently he surrenders now
Into a peaceful drowse;
Melinda keeps her dulcet watch
Lest feverish he should rouse.

And somewhere up above the clouds
That pour so hard their rains,
The purest starlight also weeps
For kind Melinda's pains.

Oh, if the stars, from where they sit,
Could tell but what they see:
Melinda fair may yet be spared
From grief's cold misery!

For on the meanest plank of wood
That bobs upon the tide
There clings a man whose only thought
Is of his cherished bride.

And near him there are others still
All cramped from holding fast
To shards of beams and booms and hull
And decking planks and mast.

So many miles they've drifted from
The rock that broke their ship
No single soul knows they've survived
When to the deeps she slipped.

How far the other ships were tossed!
How wildly had the sea
Flung boats of men the other side
Of mountains watery.

How hopeless seems their fate! Alas!
In dark, cold seas, soaked wet;
As wracked in chills their weakness deems
Their lives they must forget.

What voice within can rise against
Exhaustion, ache and bite?
Hypnotically, each labored pulse
Begs giving up the fight.

One voice, though faint, does Willie hear,
And thence impels his mind:
Melinda's voice, in whispered strains
Seem blowing in the wind;

Seems breathing in the gusts of rain;
Seems carried in the waves;
Seems buoyancy itself as the
Next crashing swell he braves.

How far to land? He cannot tell.
This night they should have docked.
This night he should have lit a fire
And with Melinda talked.

But now? No land, no fire, no ship,
Save ragged scrap of wood;
But faith! He hears Melinda yet,
Though knows not how he could.

Knows not; knows naught; knows nothing more
Than rise and fall and heave,
And grip of frozen fingers fast
And will to yet believe.

"Oh sing to me, memories sweet,
As oft she's always sung;
Without her how could I endure
This gotterdammerung?"*

All 'round him men are losing hope,
He hears them breathe goodbyes,
He hears their final parting prayers
Or cursings at the skies;

"Land ho!" he cries, he calls the names
Of men about to slip
Below into their watery graves
But for his lie's fresh grip.

"Look there!" he puts within their mind
A doubt; uncertainty;
Unsure of death, they can't succumb
To its despondency.

Ahead of them a bank of clouds
Looks near enough like land;
The sea 'twixt it and them appears
In hours could be spanned.

"A short time, now; keep steady, lads,"
Young Willie carries on;
He knows not why he has such faith
Their souls will see the dawn.

He knows not why, he knows not how
Such strength within him dwells
To hold him firmly to his life
Though flung among the swells.

Except that he can hear her voice
And so he cannot leave;
He cannot drop beneath the tide
But must survive this eve.

And just before the break of day
The storm clouds slide apart;
Then shines a moon as full as love
Upon all waking hearts.

Melinda sees it from their room
And Willie from the sea;
As if the moon is but a mirror
The other each can see.

Melinda's lips smile full, then purse:
Can she believe the thought
That Willie yet will come to her?
Has grief delusion brought?

The stars, the clouds, the moon, the rains
All hear young Willie's cry:
"Melinda, I'll ne'er yield, my love;
So long as you are nigh."

Melinda feels the flush of joy
That hope rekindled brings;
Her voice has strength, despite the hour,
As louder now she sings;

For somewhere deeper than all doubt
She senses Willie's love
Is pulsing from his living heart
Though knows she not whereof.

She knows not why, she knows not how
This sureness seems so right;
Yet knows she but to trust her soul
In matters recondite.

Now Willie sees the bank of clouds
Is land, just as he'd said;
And soon enough they'll be aground,
And not one of them dead.

It is his own dear island's shores
That reach now to enfold
Her sons, bedraggled, weary, but
More glad than can be told.

Each one of them allows his hands
To dig into the sand,
Confirming to his shaken mind
The feeling of firm land;

While spies a sun arising on
A day of such relief!
Its golden glow dispels the dark,
Dispersing clouds of grief.

But though safe from the ocean's maul
They can't escape the waves
Of raw emotions crashing through
Each one's interior caves;

For who can live beside one's death
For hours, unaffected?
Sore clearly 'fore each mind appears
Dear treasures long neglected.

"I must embrace my children," sobs
One man long out at sea;
"I never knew what mattered most
'Til near lost, utterly."

Each one sees plainly, in the hush
Of calm and glowing morn,
The ways to live their lives anew,
Spared death and soft reborn.

Hark! now from high upon a hill
A watch bell cleaves the air
See how the rescuers descend
T'administer their care;

Look close upon their eyes amazed
To see these men alive!
Each rescuer's realty 's changed
To see such storms survived!

Melinda hears the watch bell's peal;
Its meaning's crystal clear:
That she will live in love's embrace -
Dear Willie's very near!

Melinda keeps her vigil, still,
Close to the lad asleep;
She waits and watches from the door
As silent tears she weeps.

Before the sun has risen high
His silhouette she sees
Then feels herself within his arms
As both fall to their knees;

What words can tell the heart's full range
Of feelings so profound
To have young Willie in her arms --
She scarcely makes a sound;

Nor does he try to tell her now
It's her that saved his life;
He just contents himself to hold
His cherished, precious wife.

And later when the lad's revived
They bring him to his home
Across the mountains in which, lost,
For days the lad had roamed.

And then upon another street
The same silent scene unfolds
As two more souls reach not for words
But each the other holds.

Yes, all across the island flows
A quiet tide of bliss
As hearts and lives are joined again
In deepest happiness;

And who could know that grace had come
To restore futures bright
Because one heart had chose to love
Though hope was not in sight?

*gotterdammerung - a disasterous conclusion, an apocolyptic scene, an end of the world (from Norse Mythology).